THE PRE-MED LIFESTYLE

An interactive guidebook
for navigating life as a premedical student.

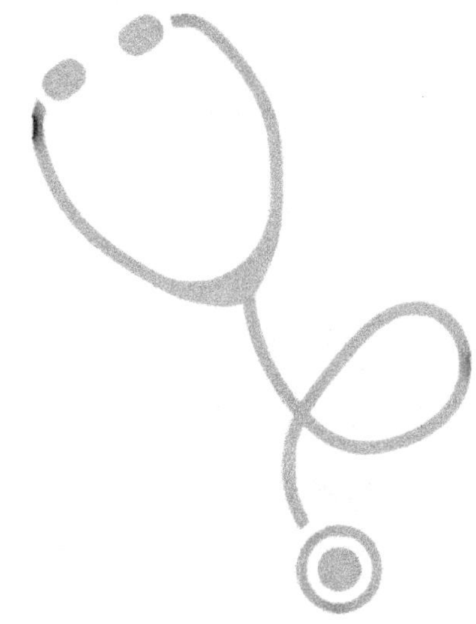

Osaro Obanor

Legal Notes

The advice and strategies contained in this book may not be suitable for your situation. It is only provided to prepare you for the pre-medical journey while outlining the experience of the early steps to pursuing a career in medicine. Readers are advised to apply their judgment about their circumstances and to act accordingly.

Dedication

To my sweet mother, who pulled me aside one evening in sixth grade and asked me what I wanted to be in life. When I told her I wanted to be a doctor, she smiled and said "Are you sure? Whether you want to be a doctor or an exotic dancer, just be truthful now so we can plan on how you can be the best at whatever you wish to do in life. Because failing to plan is making a plan to fail." That moment has stuck with me, and I appreciate unconditional love and willingness to help your friends and family reach their own goals even when it means sacrificing your own. Thank you.

To my father, for teaching me to persevere in the face of adversity and to strive on despite the opinions of naysayers. You instilled a sense of determination and resilience in our family and for these early life lessons I thank you.

Contents

Identification Page

"Today I'm just _________, but tomorrow I'll be Dr. _________."

#ClaimIt

Welcome to The Pre-Med Lifestyle!

This interactive guidebook showcases a down-to-earth approach to navigating life as a pre-medical student. Learn the ins and outs of the pre-medical journey and some helpful tips and advice to avoid common pitfalls along the way. Plan for your future and start taking steps towards success with this book in hand. Remember, the requirements to secure that admissions letter may be universal, *but everyone's journey is uniquely different.* So, stop trying to fit the "perfect pre-med" mold and start creating #ThePremedLifestyle that works for you!

How to Use This Guide?

- Read through this book to understand the steps of the pre-medical journey.
- Work through the exercises and planner structures that are included in this book to develop, grow, and set yourself up for success!
- Learn how to plan your pre-med journey from points brought up in the guide and create your own master schedule.
- Utilize the reflection exercises to develop thoughts on key concepts that are integral to becoming a medical student.
- Understand the requirements of the pre-med journey to pave a path that is uniquely your own.
- Utilize the bullet journal section to create a useful space that serves you best.

Why I Wrote This Book

Being a pre-medical student in this day and age is hard; I get it because I went through it. It doesn't just require skill and knowledge but also commitment, hard work, and the determination to seek out the opportunities and information you need to succeed. As a current fourth-year medical student and an avid promoter of mentorship, I love interacting with pre-med students to see how I can help them overcome obstacles that may manifest along their journeys to becoming a physician. I have always kept my pre-med experience in mind, which is why I hope to make your path to medicine a little less bumpy than mine was just years ago.

With the right skill set, understanding of the basics, and humility to ask for help when you need it, this journey is one any determined individual can undertake, and you will find that it can be quite fulfilling and rewarding. Helping prospective pre-med students with the steps along their journey has always given me a sense of fulfillment. My goal for you is to become the best medical school applicant you can be. I also hope that while you progress through this journey, you experience positive growth academically as well as personally. Within this guide, I take time to highlight both the academic and personal aspects of the premedical journey. I hope that with these tips and reminders that you can achieve your career goals and so much more.

Have additional questions? Need specific advice? Contact me on any social media outlet with follow-up questions or general advice. Do not hesitate to send your question using the hashtag or subject #ThePremedLifestyle because chances are many others may be searching for answers to similar questions!

Instagram/Facebook/YouTube: JustOsaroMD

Email: blazethewayorg@gmail.com

Website: www.justosaro.com

So you want to be a doctor...

Are you up for the challenge?

☐ **Yes.** ☐ **Yes.**

(no, this is not a typo)

Are you up for the challenge?

☐ **Yes.** ☐ **Yes.**

Well, the ***first step*** to mastering the pre-med lifestyle is learning that you and **only YOU** dictate your future plans. As long as you continue to **believe in yourself** and remember that success is your only option, then you are already well on your way to living out your dreams.

Remember:

It is not *"if"* you reach your goals, but *when*.

Build Your Foundation

Build Your Foundation:

It is always important to have a strong mindset and solid foundation no matter what goals you are striving to achieve. The next step towards reaching your goals are to clearly define them and then start believing in them. The answers you generate now will also be helpful for your future medical school applications. So let's get started!

What are your future goals?

1. ____
2. ____
3. ____
4. ____
5. ____

In 10 years, you would like to:

____

____

____

____

____

Build Your Foundation:

What are your inner fears?

1. ______________________________

   ____

2. ______________________________

   ____

3. ______________________________

   ____

What brings you joy?

1. ______________________________
2. ______________________________
3. ______________________________

What do you like to do for fun?

1. ______________________________
2. ______________________________
3. ______________________________

Dear Future Self

Dear Future Self: Positive Affirmations

She was unstoppable not because she did not have failures or doubts, but because she persisted on in spite of them.

–Beau Taplin

This Daily Mantra has been saved on my phone's lock screen since I went through the stressful period of studying for my first major board licensing exam. Sometimes along this journey you'll need to dig deep to find the strength and motivation to continue on ... and that is OKAY. Do yourself a favor and leave some love, inspiration, and positive vibes for your future self below. You never know when you'll need it. ☺

1) ______________________________

2) ______________________________

3) ______________________________

4) ______________________________

5) ______________________________

6) ______________________________

7) ______________________________

8) ______________________________

9) ______________________________

10) ______________________________

Dear Future Self: Positive Affirmations

My Daily Mantra

____

____

____

Dear Future Self: Positive Affirmations

Write a letter to your future self about your premedical journey

Dear____

Sincerely,

Your Pre-Med Journey Begins

Your Pre-Med Journey Begins

WHY MEDICINE?

Your answer today _/_/20_:

____

____

____

____

____

Why choose a career in medicine? This is a question that will cross the mind of every aspiring physician, whether you're just beginning your pre-medical journey or finally reaching that goal of matriculating to medical school. Although the pre-med journey is quite different for everyone, there are certain aspects of this journey that everyone battles with. Everyone possesses a unique story that inspired or motivated them to pursue a career in medicine, and their path of triumphs and struggles along the way are just as unique. For some, making the big decision to be pre-med may have come quite easy, while for others, it may have been a struggle every step of the way. It is important that you find your answer to the question "Why medicine?", not only because you will be asked this when applying and interviewing for medical school admission, but also because *remembering your "why"* will be a source of motivation and a grounding thought for you when things inevitably become stressful.

Pursuing a career in medicine is a big decision that not only affects what you will be studying in years to come, but it is a commitment to being a lifelong learner that requires many sacrifices along the way. Many people consider the time commitment, financial burden, and the academic rigor when trying to make their decision to pursue a career in medicine. In addition to thinking about these external factors, it is arguably more important to consider what your internal motivation and main driving factors are for your career choice. Take a moment to think about your answer to the question "Why medicine?" and consider your true driving factors for pursing medicine. When you have these reasons in mind, write them out below.

Your Top 5 Reasons for Pursuing a Career in Medicine:

1) ______________________________

2) ______________________________

3) ______________________________

4) ______________________________

5) ______________________________

Now that you have written out your reasons, go over them a second time. I have listed reasons below that should not be your **main** reasons for being pre-med. If they are ... you might want to think long and hard about your motivations for choosing this lifelong career.

Reasons Why You SHOULD NOT Pursue Medicine

1. For the money.
2. Because your parents/family/whoever wants you to
3. For the prestige

REMEMBER:

- The pay is good but not that great starting out as a resident physician; when you're working 24 hour shifts and missing birthdays and weddings, money won't be enough of a motivator if you don't love what you're doing.
- Your parents will not be the ones making the continuous sacrifices to become a doctor, the burden will always be only yours to carry.
- Lastly, there are many traditional and unconventional ways to be viewed as a "prestigious" member of society, so having the title of "Dr.___" is nice, but it is only one of the many respectable careers you can pursue.

Just make sure you're going into medicine for the right reasons or you run the risk of burning out or becoming dissatisfied with your career choices and the sense of delayed gratification. So think deep and really find your answer to that pivotal question: "why medicine?"

Having Trouble?

It is sometimes difficult to take the leap of faith and voice your commitment to embarking on *and* continuing the premedical journey. I just want to let you know that this hesitancy is normal. Many people struggle with finding their "why", and the rigor of being pre-med can easily make other life careers look so much more appealing. If you are trying to figure out if medicine is truly for you, go out and experience it firsthand. If you are concerned about time passing you by and how much more fun college or life in general could be without the pre-med stress, then do some reflecting and figure out ways to incorporate fun and excitement into your day while still balancing your studies. If your family wants you to pursue medicine, but your heart is not in it, then you need to seriously think about what you want out of life and start having that open dialogue with your family early on because holding those thoughts in will only cause an internal dilemma that may affect your grades and personal life without you even realizing.

Once you have done some soul searching and the proper research to declare your pursuit of a career in medicine, now is the time to seek out information, find useful resources, identify helpful people, and surround yourself with the positive support system that you need to not only be pre-med but excel at it.

Your Pre-Med Journey Begins

THE PRE-MED FORMULA?

Grades + Experience + MCAT= Admission ... right?

Many aspiring pre-medical students make the mistake of believing that there is a basic success formula for a pre-med student, but this belief is far from the truth. Success is subjective. To you, success could be having a great MCAT score, having the best mentors, publishing your own research, or simply getting into medical school. No matter what success means to you, you must strive for it without having anyone else define what it should mean to you. I can't give you a sure-fire formula for success as a pre-med student, but I can give you some advice to help you along the way. Your greatest level of success will ultimately come when you genuinely find yourself within this pre-medical journey!

Yes, everyone wants to excel as a pre-med student, and everyone wants to get admission to medical school and strive to be the best future physician they can be, but still, there is no such thing as the "ideal pre-medical student." I say this because being pre-med is not simply completing a series of checklists that ends with you scoring a medical school admission letter. True, there are premedical requirements, but the premedical journey is much more than a task list for completion; it is designed to cultivate the necessary personal and professional growth of future physicians prior to them beginning their medical training. So through each academic requirement, clinical experience, and research endeavor, the focus is just as much on what you learned from each experience in addition to the actual achievement itself.

When embarking on this journey to a career in medicine, it is important to recognize that our differences are what make us unique. Your experience on this journey will be unique to you because we all will take slightly different paths and have different interests and passions that motivate and fulfill us along the way. These differences are what will make the classes of medical schools more diverse and, in many ways, are among the most important characteristics sought out of potential future physicians.

Thus, you must learn to embrace your uniqueness and focus on learning who you truly are. You may have some rough patches along the way but just continue to *believe in yourself* and *trust the process*. The best thing you can do for yourself at any stage of your pre-med journey is to understand yourself and what works best for you. I am being a bit of a hypocrite when I stress this point as this was actually my least favorite piece of advice that I heard from almost every medical student I encountered during my undergraduate years. As a pre-med student, I wanted to know the secrets to success and the tips and tricks I seemed to be missing when comparing myself to the infamous trolls posting on the pre-med corners of the internet. But in reality, the most repeated piece of advice I received was to know yourself, take time to figure out how you learn best, and ALWAYS make it a priority to take care of yourself. As not helpful as it may have seemed then, now that I am on the other side of things, I could not agree more with this advice. When you know yourself and can acknowledge your strengths and weaknesses and highlight the things that make you unique, you not only expand your presence, but you will be able to cultivate a version of yourself that will withstand the rigors of this journey to a career in medicine. So learn to embrace your uniqueness and be at peace with who you are. You might not be exactly where you want to be just yet but trust the process and look forward to where you are heading next.

What are your strengths?

1) ______________________________

2) ______________________________

3) ______________________________

4) ______________________________

5) ______________________________

What are your biggest weaknesses?

1) ______________________________

2) ______________________________

3) ____

How can these weaknesses be improved to eventually become a strength?

1) ____

____

2) ____

____

3) ____

____

Your Unique Journey

Regardless of what your strengths and weaknesses may be, medical schools want to know what makes us all unique and sets us apart from the pack. Please don't worry about trying to fit that template of the ideal "cookie cutter" pre-med student because it is your extra edges and curves that will ultimately enhance your individual story and pique the interest of admission committees. Your chances of doing so are better when you stand out uniquely and highlight the attributes that define who you are as a person. So take the time to understand yourself and your strengths and weaknesses as you spend time doing the things you truly have passion for the most. Passion and authenticity are very important characteristics for success as a pre-med student. When you learn to move at your own pace and get involved with things you enjoy, you will not only perform well; but you will also be motivated to continue seeking higher achievements in these endeavors. Work towards success and progress on your terms and don't let pressures from anyone define or change what is truly important to you.

Which characteristics best describe you? (circle 3)

Humble	Enthusiastic	Confident	Caring
Determined	Creative	Reliable	Social
Inquisitive	Hardworking	Adaptive	Selfish
Stubborn	Timid	Aggressive	Defensive
Talkative	Supportive	Funny	Perfectionist

It's best to figure out the path you want to take as early as possible because this will help you plan and create a pre-med journey that suits your lifestyle and overall goals.

Becoming a pre-med student is not supposed to change your way of life completely, but rather, it is meant to add on to it. So you don't have to completely lose who you are because of your desire to become a medical student. The essence of your journey in medicine is to contribute meaningfully to the lives of others while staying true to who you really are. Unfortunately, many students who start this journey find it very difficult to keep up with it, not because they are not self-motivated or intellectually capable, but more so because they no longer believed their goals were attainable. On my college move-in day, I remember vividly how the pre-medical dean told a room full of eager pre-med students that only one third of us would make it through college as a pre-med, and even fewer of us would go on to make it to medical school. This created not only an air of competition, but it also created a feeling of self-doubt and worry among even the smartest of my classmates. Thus, it is important to believe in yourself and to plan out how you are going to attain your goals. This will help your journey seem much more manageable as the first steps to success are having the right mindset and finding the right tools.

Your success is dependent on how you tailor your pre-med journey to fit your lifestyle and personality. Along the journey to medicine, it is true that you will have many sacrifices, but it is important to hold on to the things in your life that are core to who you are today. Consider your priorities and make a list of things you can't compromise on as you go through your pre-medical journey. Understand your values, make a blueprint of your non-negotiables, and find a way to make it work harmoniously with your life as a pre-med student. Start making this list below ... I took the liberty of filling the first two out for you!

The List of Non-Negotiables:

- Self-Care
- "The 3 S's" Sleep, Study, and Social Life ... Myth: you cannot have all three. Fact: you can ... it just takes some work. ☺
- ____
- ____
- ____
- ____
- ____

Pursuing medicine will certainly feel difficult if you are struggling with tailoring your premed journey to fit your lifestyle. Having a balanced life while you are on this journey will not only lead to success, but it will also make your journey *feel* less stressful. A balanced life as a pre-med student is a good recipe for personal wellness, and trust me, you will need it!

Many students get so caught up with classes, assignments, and deadlines that they forget to prioritize personal wellness. One would think as the rising members of the future of healthcare, we would care most about this, but the sad reality is that many students and physicians neglect their wellness for the sake of intense learning, completing assignments, and meeting deadlines to bring their goal of caring for others to fruition. This unconscious negligence is one of the many contributing factors to things such as chronic stress, burn-out, sleep deprivation, anxiety, depression, and suicide that occur at alarming rates among pre-meds, medical students, and practicing physicians alike. *So....*

I urge you to begin to consciously ***tend to your personal wellness*** *as it is vital that you develop the* ***resilience*** *needed to thrive in your career in medicine and* ***maintain your own wellbeing*** *in order to best serve others.*

Planning for Your Pre-Med Journey

Planning for Your Pre-med Journey

Choosing to pursue a career in medicine is a long-term commitment to service and considering the needs of others first—sometimes even above your own. Although the journey to becoming a physician is quite long, the feeling of impacting people's lives in such a personal way is undoubtedly quite rewarding. But the path to becoming a physician is time-consuming, highly competitive, and very tedious. If you have decided on a career in medicine, this choice commits you to roughly seven to ten years of additional education and training after college and a lifelong commitment of being a physician learner. Before we start planning the specifics of your pre-med journey, let's review an overall outline of the pre-medical pathway.

The Pre-Medical Trajectory: A Quick Refresher

High School:

You must first graduate from high school, and it is best to graduate with the highest grades possible, as well as to engage in a variety of activities that show leadership, teamwork, and an appreciable balance of interest. Having an excellent GPA from high school is also equally important. The higher your GPA, and the more you participate and excel in extracurricular activities, the better your chances are of getting accepted into colleges of your choice. If you also have the opportunity to take advanced classes, particularly in math or science, it will enhance your chances once you begin your medical school applications.

College:

After graduating from high school, you must also graduate from college and complete the necessary pre-medical undergraduate courses if you are hoping to pursue a career in medicine. Your undergraduate years are meant to prepare you academically for your medical school education, but it is also a time for you to explore and learn new things both related to and completely different from the field of medicine. Amidst your exploration of life and pursuit of knowledge, your pre-med years should be utilized as a time to set a foundational plan toward getting accepted into the medical school of your choice. It is very important during these years to plan ahead and stay on track with your general coursework and pre-med requirements.

Pre-med students who do well academically tend to plan early. Not planning ahead of time is one of the most common obstacles most pre-med students face. It is important to map out your task plans early enough to avoid unnecessary pitfalls. Know the courses you are going to take for each semester and have a good plan towards excelling in them. It shouldn't come as a surprise that a strong academic performance in your pre-medical years is a crucial factor in your acceptance into medical school. Too often, pre-med students fail to actualize their goal of getting into medical school as a result of improper planning. Poor academic performance in pre-medical school is not entirely based on intellectual incapacity; sometimes it is as a result of some strategic mistakes. Some students make the mistake of taking too many pre-med or core classes in the same semester, and they end up underperforming. Carrying on more workload than you can handle is a big recipe for disaster, no matter how smart or good your intentions are. No matter how hard you think you can work, it is not realistic to perform excellently in organic chemistry, biostatistics, biology, and physics all at the same time while balancing a social life and a full load of extracurricular activities.

Remember:

Balance your course schedule with core and elective classes

It is good to be realistic when setting milestones that you want to achieve in each pre-medical year. Medical schools do want to see that you were able to handle multiple rigorous courses despite their obvious difficulties, but there is no need to bite off more than you can chew. Personally, I'd advise you to take two difficult science/core courses each semester or quarter and balance it out with one or two elective courses that require less time so that you can take full advantage of office hours and perform well in the lab components all while maintaining your extracurriculars.

Figure out a way to effectively balance your academic work with your social life. Yes, the road to becoming a physician is a long one, but it doesn't have to be entirely boring. Try your best to get involved with college activities as much as possible, as it will not only be a great break from studying, but it will also represent who you are outside of the classroom in your medical school applications. It is important to take up some extracurricular activities but be careful not to overload your schedule. Most pre-med students often think the more extracurriculars you engage in, the higher your chances of getting in are, but this is far from the truth. It is important to stay balanced with just enough activities that you enjoy and excel in without having to compromise your academics. Medical admission committees pay more attention to your overall GPA and the *quality* of your activities rather than the number of things that you participated in. To medical schools, how well you perform in your pre-med years is indicative of how ready you are to perform at the level of rigor and organization that medical school requires.

Creating the right plan for your situation sets you up for success. Of course, you might end up making significant changes to your plan as you go through your pre-medical years, but having a general idea of your overall academic plan as you begin your pre-med journey will prevent you from having to scramble to finish your prerequisites or recommended courses later on when it comes closer to application time. Make sure you work closely with your pre-med advisors or a mentor during your pre-med years as they will help you to create a plan that sets you up to be ready to apply by your intended timeline.

A major part of creating a plan is setting up an accurate timeline. Some pre-med students plan to start their medical school applications immediately during their senior year, while some applicants are open to the option of taking the gap year before putting together their medical school application. This decision is entirely subjective as it purely depends on what works best for you. If you are wondering what a gap year really means, it basically refers to the period of time between the end of your pre-medical undergraduate years and the start of medical school. A gap year is the time taken off between college and medical school which can be a single year or multiple depending on the specific situation and what works best for each student.

Before you decide whether taking a gap year is best for you, you need to analyze your motivations and determine how strong your medical application is. Some applicants are "ready" by graduation, so taking a gap year before commencing their medical school applications might just seem like an unnecessary delay to them. I think it is important to address that needing or desiring a gap year does not make an applicant less competitive and does not speak to your performance ability. Students actually choose to add a gap year into their pathway for a multitude of reasons and the list of why's are quite long.

What are some strategic reasons why people choose a gap year? Well, the gap year path is sometimes advised if you are looking to boost your chances of getting into medical school by taking the time to enhance weaker areas of your application. A gap year could be the perfect opportunity for you to improve your MCAT score, finish up any missing prerequisites, supplement a low GPA with a science-based masters or post baccalaureate program, volunteer in a medically-related field, or gain some research experience. Some students even opt for a gap year to take an emotional or mental break from academics, to reflect on long-term goals, or to pursue a totally different career. It is also used by some as an opportunity to gear up financially for the journey ahead (exams, applications, and interviews all cost money $$$).

But whichever way you decide to ultimately spend your possible gap year(s), use some of that time to reflect and make sure you are really ready to start your journey towards a career in medicine. Check out the next few pages of tasks to keep in mind as you progress through your premed journey. Feel free to amend these items to more accurately match your intended pre-med timeline.

Year-by-Year Breakdown

Freshman Year:

- Look up Pre-Medical requirements on www.aamc.org and find out your institution's specific requirements (they may or may not be the same).
- Seek out and meet with your pre-health advisor EARLY.
- Get settled to life in college and learn how you study best.
- Start thinking about what major you want to pursue and begin planning your course schedule outline to the best of your knowledge.
- Get INVOLVED! Join enriching organizations like AMSA Premed Section and SNMA/MAPS, as well as other non-academic groups on campus.
- Find your tribe; meet other pre-meds, form study groups, and create a support system of your peers.

Sophomore Year:

- Confirm your major and update your course schedule outline with both your pre-med and major/graduation requirements.
- Continue to meet with your pre-health advisor at least once a year.
- Monitor your grades, general GPA, AND calculate your science GPA.
- Get involved and STAY involved with extracurricular activities.
- Identify and pursue leadership opportunities on campus.
- Start and continue a log of hours/descriptions of your activities and a running draft of a CV/resume.
- Find mentors who care (important).
- Actively seek out summer experiences.

Junior Year:

- Continue to meet with pre-health advisor.
- Continue to grow your support system.
- Connect with the pre-health office and figure out if your school uses "committee letter" format for letters of recommendation for medical school applications.
- Attend any on-campus sessions regarding to applying to medical school and do your own research on the topic as well: Check out AAMC, webinars, blogs, StudentDoctorNet (with a grain of salt ^.^).
- Ask for <u>STRONG</u> recommendation letters from trusted professors or other faculty you have worked with (Ask EARLY, as some teachers have limited space).

- Figure out your timeline for applying and when applicable, complete these steps by the summer before:
    - Plan for, study, and take the MCAT
    - Write, re-write, and edit a personal statement.
    - Begin filling in AMCAS (application opens late spring for applicants to begin filling portions out).
    - Gather letters of recommendation and/or committee letters

- Set aside money or method of payment for the AMCAS general application and secondary fees.
- Begin to budget money for interview season based on how many interviews you set a goal for.

Senior Year:

<u>If Actively Applying:</u>

- Submit your applications early in the summer. Interviews are offered on a rolling basis after application review is underway, so don't wait until the deadlines to submit!
- Send reminder emails to make sure all of your letters of recommendations have been sent in a timely manner.
- Plan your schedule wisely since you will be interviewing during the fall and winter months.
- Enjoy interview season and make sure to have some fun between school and interviews so you don't burn out!

FINISH OUT THE YEAR STRONG! It's #GradSZN

Gap Year

- Make a timeline for your gap year plans, set goals early, and carve out an outline of how you'll spend your time.
- Also reach out to potential letter writers early so they don't forget you!

FINISH OUT THE YEAR STRONG! Its #GradSZN

Remember:

It is never too late to adopt a good strategy for a successful pre-med journey. Understand the term balance and learn to readdress your priorities. Learn to face each stage gracefully and avoid overestimating your competitiveness. Always remember, with the right plan, you'll be able to easily navigate your way, no matter how difficult it might seem!

The Basics:

Pre-Med Requirements

The Basics: Pre-Med Requirements

Be Proactive and Stay Informed

To avoid misdirection, it's best to get the facts straight before you start your application. As luck will have it, there is a wealth of information and opportunities available to pre-medical students that can ease your pathway to medical school. The smart choices and decisions you make throughout this journey will heavily contribute to securing an admission, and you cannot make these choices effectively if you are not well informed.

Remember:

Your pre-med preparations should start as early possible.

If you are still in high school, and you are considering a career as a medical practitioner, now is your best time to begin taking baby steps toward fulfilling your dreams. It is advisable to take college preparatory courses and as much science and math that is available in your school. Your efforts should be projected towards getting excellent grades in the science and math courses available to you. It is also important that you participate in extracurricular activities. Volunteering in a medical setting is a perfect idea, and getting involved in any activity that you not only enjoy doing but that also shows your commitment to helping people is fantastic.

Your pre-med journey can also begin during or after your college years.

This journey can begin at any point in your life, and it is entirely up to you to decide when you want to start. Although medical schools have course requirements for admission, when it comes to your major, what you study is up to you. The point here is that your major is not as important as your GPA. Students have majored in non-science related fields or pursued entirely different careers and still gotten accepted into great medical schools. Thus, whenever you do decide to start your premed journey, it is important to keep in mind that most schools pay special attention to your science GPA and it is essential to keep your grades up in science-related courses from that point on.

Many students may prepare for med school right after college but recently, many pre-med applicants find the idea of taking a gap year before they begin their applications quite appealing and enter into the "non-traditional" pathway. The appeal for a gap year centers on an applicant's ability to become a stronger candidate academically, financially, and even emotionally. Like I previously mentioned, whether you choose to observe a gap year and how you decide to spend it is up to you, but it is important to be aware of all of your options and pathways available to you. Stay updated about the various pathways and keep a lookout for new ways that may arise to strengthen yourself as a premedical student.

Passing the MCAT is essential to your premedical journey.

As a pre-med student, another item to plan and prepare for is how to achieve your best results on the MCAT. At this stage, you may be confused by the mystery behind the MCAT exam and worried about what the exam is all about. The MCAT is the acronym of the Medical College Admission Test, and it is an essential requirement for your admission into medical school. The Association of American Medical Colleges administers the exam, and it is essentially designed to assess your problem solving and critical thinking skill, as well as your knowledge of natural, behavioral, and social science concepts and principles. Since my goal is to make this journey less stressful for you, the first thing you should do is stop worrying about the MCAT exam being difficult. Speaking from personal experience, I would say MCAT exam is difficult, not because of the extensive subject matter but because it is your first major exam that requires you to be prepared both emotionally and academically. Because of this, you must formulate a plan and stay organized in order to conquer the MCAT.

It is important to figure out *when* you want to take your MCAT exam and to carve out your ideal study time in preparation for success. Generally, the MCAT exam is offered January through September, and there are about 25 MCAT dates to choose from.

Regardless of this window of opportunity available to you, it is very important that you take the MCAT exam as early in the year as possible and, in my opinion, no later than June since AMCAS application submissions begin in early June. Although there are no direct consequences attached to waiting until as late as early September before taking your MCAT test, you should bear in mind that MCAT scores are released about a month after the test date and many schools will not look at your application until your MCAT scores are available.

Plan to start your exam preparations ASAP because completing the exam earlier will allow you to complete your AMCAS application early; and the earlier you submit your application, the better. There is also the looming question of what resources are best to prepare for the MCAT. I am a huge fan of MCAT prep courses. It is also possible to self-study for the MCAT but it is imperative to not only purchase practice exams but to also purchase some sort of content review package. So read reviews on dedicated MCAT courses from Kaplan or Princeton Review or purchase content review book sets to craft your study plan.

The Basics: Pre-Med Requirements

Academics

A vital key to medical admission success is careful and strategic planning based on correct information. To make the most of your pre-med journey, it is important to be well informed on the academic requirements expected of you. Accurate information prevents pitfalls and delayed timelines. It's never too early to research the basic academic requirements of specific medical schools that you are interested in. Academic advisors, pre-health officers, program directors, and counselors are all people who may be able to be valuable sources of information but do not always rely on their advice.

Find the right course load and maintaining academic balance is very important at this stage. Meeting the required academic requirements on time pretty much determines whether your application gets considered or is just automatically filtered out to the trash, so it's best to work with the most up-to-date information. Premedical requirements can change from year to year or vary from school to school but there are general requirements that remain constant. You can find the basic academic requirements which applicants must meet during their pre-med years online and this can serve as a starting point for creating your academic plan. On the next page, I have listed a basic outline of pre-med requirements.

The basic outline of **pre-medical requirements** includes:

- One Year of Biology
- One Year of General Chemistry + Lab
- One Year of Physics + Lab
- One Year of Organic Chemistry + Lab
- Psychology
- Sociology
- Math (Calculus)
- Statistics
- Biochemistry
- Extracurricular Activities
- Clinical/Medical Exposure/Volunteer /Research Experiences
- MCAT Exam
- Recommendation Letters
- Completed AMCAS Application

These requirements are a basic outline of pre-med requisites and may vary according to the specific academic requirements of the medical school you are applying to. Some schools may have additional requirements or specific courses, like a genetics class, that are among their internal requirements for admission. I recommended that you check with each medical school that you may want to apply to and the AAMC because requirements can and do change.

Crafting a working outline of your course schedule ahead of time will allow you to create a manageable pre-med schedule and have flexibility as your plan things like study time to prepare for the MCAT, study abroad opportunities, research, and internships. Let's take a quick look at a possible schedule formatted for a basic pre-medical student's undergraduate curriculum:

**** It is important to note that AP Credits will allow you to "sub out" some of the prerequisite courses that may be listed in this sample schedule. AP Credit offering differs from school to school so please research your institutions policy as well as checking with the AAMC's general and specific medical schools' premedical requisites.

Sample Premedical Schedule (with no AP Credits)

	Fall Semester	Spring Semester	Summer
First Year	-Chemistry 1 -Math (usually calculus) -General Course (GC) -Foreign Language (FL) 1	-Chemistry 2 -GC -GC -English/ writing Course	*Possible Science course * Internship *SHPEP summer health experience
Second Year	- Chemistry 2 -Biology 101 -FL 2 -GC	-Organic Chemistry 1 -Biology 102 -Psychology -GC	*Study Abroad
Third Year	-Organic Chemistry 2 -Physics 1 -Statistics -GC	-Physics 2 -Biochem -Sociology -GC *MCAT prep	*MCAT prep *MCAT May/June *Applications in June *Study Abroad
Fourth Year	-GC -GC -GC -GC *interviewing	-GC -GC -GC -GC *interviewing	
*Summer sessions may also be used to complete additional coursework which can free up your schedule during the year if needed.			

This curriculum is only recommended, and you don't have to follow this framework. However, it is important to create a plan to follow. It's ideal to plan towards taking no more than two laboratory courses per semester and avoid overloading too many laboratory courses in one semester.

Since I am a big proponent of planning out your course schedules ahead of time, I have taken the time to create the 4 Year Course Schedule planning sheet. This schedule planning sheet is perfect for the pre-professional student and will help you visualize your academic to-do list and makes it very easy to make changes to your schedule and your long term premedical plans as a whole. On the following two pages you can find my custom schedule planner and additional printables can be found online on my website, www.justosaro.com

Happy Planning!

The 4 - Year Course Schedule

Freshman Year

Fall 20

	Requirement Met
Course 1	Gen Pre Maj
Course 2	Gen Pre Maj
Course 3	Gen Pre Maj
Course 4	Gen Pre Maj
Course 5	Gen Pre Maj

Important To do for Semester

- [ ]
- [ ]
- [ ]
- [ ]

Spring 20

	Requirement Met
Course 1	Gen Pre Maj
Course 2	Gen Pre Maj
Course 3	Gen Pre Maj
Course 4	Gen Pre Maj
Course 5	Gen Pre Maj

Important To do for Semester

- [ ]
- [ ]
- [ ]
- [ ]

Summer Plans

Sophomore Year

Fall 20

	Requirement Met
Course 1	Gen Pre Maj
Course 2	Gen Pre Maj
Course 3	Gen Pre Maj
Course 4	Gen Pre Maj
Course 5	Gen Pre Maj

Important To do for Semester

- [ ]
- [ ]
- [ ]
- [ ]

Spring 20

	Requirement Met
Course 1	Gen Pre Maj
Course 2	Gen Pre Maj
Course 3	Gen Pre Maj
Course 4	Gen Pre Maj
Course 5	Gen Pre Maj

Important To do for Semester

- [ ]
- [ ]
- [ ]
- [ ]

Summer Plans

The 4 - Year Course Schedule

Junior Year

Fall 20

	Requirement Met
Course 1	Gen Pre Maj
Course 2	Gen Pre Maj
Course 3	Gen Pre Maj
Course 4	Gen Pre Maj
Course 5	Gen Pre Maj

Important To do for Semester

- [ ]
- [ ]
- [ ]
- [ ]

Spring 20

	Requirement Met
Course 1	Gen Pre Maj
Course 2	Gen Pre Maj
Course 3	Gen Pre Maj
Course 4	Gen Pre Maj
Course 5	Gen Pre Maj

Important To do for Semester

- [ ]
- [ ]
- [ ]
- [ ]

Summer Plans

Senior Year

Fall 20

	Requirement Met
Course 1	Gen Pre Maj
Course 2	Gen Pre Maj
Course 3	Gen Pre Maj
Course 4	Gen Pre Maj
Course 5	Gen Pre Maj

Important To do for Semester

- [ ]
- [ ]
- [ ]
- [ ]

Spring 20

	Requirement Met
Course 1	Gen Pre Maj
Course 2	Gen Pre Maj
Course 3	Gen Pre Maj
Course 4	Gen Pre Maj
Course 5	Gen Pre Maj

Important To do for Semester

- [ ]
- [ ]
- [ ]
- [ ]

Summer Plans

The Basics: Pre-Med Requirements

Choosing A Major

So many pre-med students are faced with the question of which major will best increase their chances of getting into medical school. As much as your choice of major affects your academic performance, it is important to remember that your major doesn't matter nearly as much to medical admission committees as your GPA. What you decide to major in during your pre-med years is entirely up to you, although you must meet the basic admission requirements regardless of your choice. Deciding to take up a major in biological sciences in does not increase your chances of getting into medical school compared to someone who majors in anthropology. The point is that you don't have to feel restricted to majoring in a hard science. Do what you love and what feels right for you!

Since special attention is paid to your science GPA, it is best to choose a pre-med major in something that truly interests you and that you think you can excel in, rather than merely what you think med schools want to see. There is no point taking up a major that you are not interested in because you believe it may boost your chances of getting into med school. In the long run, it may adversely affect your grades as you may have a hard time keeping up with a major that you are not passionate about. Once you have decided on a major, obtain the curriculum from the department and evaluate the program through all four years of its requirements. Know the courses, prerequisites, and core requisites for each semester. It is very important that you understand the sequence of the courses required to obtain the degree and how well the pre-med courses fit into or alongside your chosen major.

Make a mental note to plan for your required courses and try to keep up with them. Like I've earlier mentioned, planning is a vital tool for success as a pre-med student. Choose to tackle the courses that are required most by medical schools first. It is advisable to develop a curriculum that you can easily work with all through your pre-med years. You can seek the help of your pre-med advisor or mentor while you are planning your courses. He or she can help create a successful roadmap specific to your institution. Don't make the mistake of selecting courses without direction; this may end up hurting you in the long run. Create and settle upon an academic strategy that will outline your schedule of courses—not just for your first semester but for the rest of the semesters as well.

The Basics: Pre-Med Requirements

Extracurricular Activities

Being well rounded is very important on the journey to becoming a physician. No one cares that you were able to keep up a high GPA in your pre-med years by just confining yourself to the classroom and your dorm room. Medical admission committees want to see that you performed well academically while also excelling in some extracurricular activities whether they be service, talent, or skill related.

What then is a good extracurricular activity? Basically, an extracurricular activity can refer to any activity outside of the classroom and your studies. It includes (but is absolutely not limited to) clinical experiences such as shadowing a physician and working in a hospital, research projects (clinical, transitional, and basic science), volunteering in the community, working a job, pursuing a hobby, and joining student organizations available at your institution. Taking up extracurricular activities as a pre-med is advisable because it contribute to your personal growth and portrays qualities such as leadership, dedication, and collaboration, which are some of the qualities medical admission committees look for in an ideal applicant. A career in medicine is all about rendering a selfless service at all times. It is one thing to say that you wish to help people as a physician, but dedicating your time and energy to a cause, an event, or a concept outside of yourself truly backs it up.

Extracurricular activities are an important component for a "complete" medical school application. Now more than ever, medical school admissions committees are putting more emphasis on recruiting students who, beyond having a strong academic background, are well balanced, well rounded and will be a good fit for their preferred medical schools. Medical admission committees want to see that you are not just another smart kid. Your extracurricular activities reflect that you are more than committed to making a difference in the life of others. When evaluating a student's application, admission committees look for certain traits like altruism, compassion, and empathy that shine through an applicant's words or entries. They are always on the lookout for people who care selflessly for others and are willing to make a difference since that is the sole aim of medicine after all. In order to demonstrate that you have the qualities they are in search of, you must show it through how you spend your free time.

As much as an extracurricular is a requisite for admission into medical school, it should be something born out of sheer passion and not wholly based on the fact that it will increase your chances of getting in. Pre-med extracurricular activities should be viewed as a means within themselves. So instead of asking "what extracurricular activities do pre-meds need?" ask "what extracurricular activities will develop my passion?" If you take up activities for the sheer pleasure of it, you'll ultimately give it your best; but if you only engage in extracurricular activities because you view it is a requirement, you will probably struggle to connect with it and your lack of passion will be quite visible to committees on your application and in interviews.

Since much emphasis is placed on taking up extracurricular activities, some pre-med students believe that they should "pad" their resumes with many activities to better their chances of getting in. This is a temptation that many pre-med students face because they believe that they need to "check all the boxes" to succeed. Bouncing around activities and groups during your first year is encouraged, but it is more beneficial to have a clear idea of what activities you are genuinely interested in by the time your second year is over. Aim to commit to three regular extracurricular activities to stay active with over time. Develop a connection with the activities you spend the most time doing and maybe even pursue leadership positions if you truly are invested in them. Having care and commitment over time shows admission committees that you are not just another applicant who tried to pad their resume.

Strive for balance and don't worry about whether or not you'll have enough extracurricular activities to impress medical admission committees; you should be more concerned with finding activities that speak to you and will foster meaningful experiences and outcomes. There is no point taking up many extracurricular activities if you can't express why it is meaningful to you. Your job is to make what you commit to count!

Choosing extracurricular activities that fit your lifestyle is equally important. Although there are no prescribed extracurricular activities that can guarantee you a spot in your medical school of choice, there are some types extracurricular activities that every medical school admission committee wants to see on your application. Some of these activities include:

Volunteering & Community Service:

This is one of the extracurricular activities valued by most medical school admissions committees. In a report published by the Association of American Medical Colleges (AAMC), it was admitted that after grades and letters of recommendation, an applicant's participation in medical-related community service was considered the next most important criterion in deciding not only if they will invite them to an interview but also if acceptance was offered.

Volunteering and community service not only helps to bolster your applications, but it also shows that you are ready for a life-long career in medicine. It proves that you have commitment to service and it demonstrates that you are the type of person who can dedicate time to serve without throwing in the towel no matter how difficult the odds may seem. It also can give you the opportunity to get in touch with real life medicine (free clinic, local health fairs, etc.) and helps you decide if this is really what you want to do for the rest of your life.

Finding an avenue to volunteer your services is one of the easiest things to do as there are so many channels for it. Try your local health department, habitat for humanity, or local shelters. You could volunteer at a hospital or clinic to gain broad exposure to working within a health care setting (greeters, docents, scribes, patient services volunteer); you could also volunteer as a member of a medical corps or Red Cross community teams to help assist crisis-affected communities or families in need.

Shadowing

Shadowing is another form of extracurricular activity that allows pre-meds to engage first hand with patients and observe practicing doctors work with patients. This is believed to be one of the best ways to show that you are acquainted with a career in medicine. It allows you to see what medicine and a physician's life are like every day, and admission committees believe that these experiences allow you to discover and further prove if medicine is right for you. Basically, the importance of shadowing boils down to one thing: clinical exposure. Medical admission committees want to see that you have immersed yourself in clinical settings with real patients and you have experienced medicine from the delivery aspect and not just as a patient.

Shadowing also offers you the opportunity to develop a mentorship relationship with the physician you shadowed. This will not only help make your journey easier, but it will also come in handy in terms of letters of recommendation. Getting letters of recommendation from the physicians you shadowed and had a close relationship with is way easier than getting from those who you don't have a longstanding relationship with. They are one of the best people to attest to your overall behavioral attributes and performance, even for the short time you may have worked with them. The more in-depth their testament to the type of student you are, the better their letter of recommendation will be. You can collect your recommendation letters after each shadowing experience by making use programs like of Interfolio. Interfolio allows letters of recommendation to be received and distributed electronically or on paper. This avenue is advised because your mentors may know things about you while you were shadowing with them but may not be able to recall those thoughts years later when you when you finally need recommendation letters for various opportunities.

It is never too early to start stacking up your letters of recommendation.

Leadership Experience

Most times, this activity is paid less attention by some pre-med students. Make sure to seek out leadership roles during your premedical years. Having at least one of your entries highlight work or activities that show admission committees that you are an experienced leader and team player will serve you well.

Although having a leadership experience may not seem like a big deal in the grand scheme of things, it really goes a long way in building a holistic case for why you are a stellar applicant. Many medical schools look favorably upon applicants that have held notable leadership positions during their pre-med years, and some schools actually state that applicants should have leadership experiences or service to be considered.

Research

Pre-med students who are involved in research, regardless of the study topic, often demonstrate to admission committees that they are well versed in scientific inquiry, experimental design, and in cases where the outcome is a publication, accomplished in scientific writing. Although prior research experience is not a requirement for admission into most schools, it can definitely be an advantage on your application. The reason for that is quite obvious: a research background shows off your curiosity, maturity, and work ethic – qualities of students who are prepared to handle the challenges of medical school. There are many ways to get involved in research from bench positions in a lab to assisting with ongoing psychology studies at your college. Diversify your idea of "what counts" as research and you can find a position that will work well for you!

These are just some of the many extracurricular activities that you can pick up as a pre-med, but do not restrict yourself to the more common activities on the "pre-med" list. Find an extracurricular that you are passionate about and think of how it can connect it to your future plans a medical professional. Remember, take up extracurricular activities because you care enough to spend time doing it—not just for a resume. When the time comes, you'll write about these passions organically, relate it to your journey and drive home your "reasons why" with ease.

Mentorship & Guidance

Mentorship & Guidance

In addition to getting good grades, it is equally important to expose yourself to medicine early on and to begin building your professional support system. If you are at all serious about your journey as a pre-med student, it is very important to seek the help of medical mentors or advisors. Securing mentorship, shadowing, and volunteer opportunities are things that give some pre-med students more advantages over others as they tend to be better prepared for success.

The journey through college and then to medical school is pretty difficult, even for the best college students. Medicine is already hard enough as it is, and no one can successfully become med student or a doctor existing in a vacuum. By identifying a mentor, you not only have someone who is familiar with the journey you aspire to make but you also can have a sounding board for all the potential difficulties and choices you may encounter along the way. Mentorship is all about having someone well informed to help you along your journey in a variety of contexts. Think of a mentor as someone who helps you figure things out. It could be that you needed directions on the courses to register for, grades, MCAT, volunteering, and even shadowing opportunities while preparing for your journey.

I have and still continue to benefit from having mentors. I can tell you that mentorship is more than finding an empathetic ear to listen to you; it is all about cultivating a relationship that you feel comfortable enough in to truly *ask for what you need*. Your mentor may share personal stories of both successes and mistakes that they endured along their journey but if you do not *ask* for the type of guidance or advice you need then you are doing yourself a disservice. Apart from the anecdotes and motivational benefits mentorship may offer, a medical mentor can also provide you with tangible advice like recommendations for internships and medical schools or even personal statement and application review. But not everyone can serve as a mentor and not every mentor can serve you in every capacity that you may need. Your choice for a mentor should always be someone you feel comfortable with because, without a genuine level of comfort, the goal of mentorship won't be fully realized. Find someone who not only understands what you are trying to do but also wants to help you figure things out and has the time to do so. You can also have many mentors for different aspects of your life in order to make your mentorship experiences more beneficial.

For academic guidance, your college professors are actually readily available to help you, so don't be afraid to go in office hours, talk to a Teaching Assistant (TA), or set up an appointment to go over topics that you can't quite understand. If they aren't able to clarify things as much as you want, then make the most of the internet! There are so many helpful resources online that pre-med students can look out for, such as supplemental books like "Organic Chemistry as a Second Language," online video lectures such as those from Khan Academy and Lecturio, and online pre- or self-made study aids like Quizlet. There are many ways for you to solidify your understanding of subject matter and you just need to be pointed in the right direction to find them!

It is also beneficial to have a good working relationship with your fellow pre-med students and upperclassmen. You need all the advice you can get on this journey, and working harmoniously with other people who have a similar goal as you can make finding information quite easy. Your fellow pre-med students and upperclassmen are not just a reliable source of information alone, but they are also there for emotional support and to help you through things when they get rough! No matter how good you think you are on your own, you should always welcome others to help guide you to in your time of need (*trust me*). So if you haven't made it a priority before, start thinking of ways to foster a collaborative pre-med environment to surround yourself with.

Counselors, Professors, & Advisors

Apart from sorting out your class schedule and fitting into your new environment, getting well acquainted with your professors and advisors should also be among your top priorities.

There are so many reasons why you should have a cordial relationship with your faculty and staff early on.

First off, faculty members are there as a resource to help you achieve whatever academic goal you have set out to accomplish. Your professors, advisors, and counselors can be great allies as they already know the system and can extend to you the benefit of their professional experience. They can help you along your journey by providing helpful insight and knowledge that can be beneficial to your success. They are sometimes the first people to learn about new opportunities through their professional network, so a good rapport with them could have a real impact on your academic life and career development.

Having a good relationship with these key players in your pre-med journey makes it quite easy to ask for help when you need it. Being pre-med is quite demanding, and not every class is going to go on smoothly. Having a good running relationship with your professor and TAs can help you smooth out those rougher times during the semester. It also will be much easier asking for future letters of recommendations when you already have a relationship with them.

A good working relationship with your professors and advisors can also go a long way in creating opportunities for you outside the college environment. Life continues on before, during, and after your college years, and you might need to handle things that fall outside of your premed plans such as applying for scholarships, finding internships, or securing a job. These things may require professional or academic recommendations and your relationships with college professors and advisors will definitely prove useful in such cases.

Although you can request a letter of recommendation from professors once you have completed their class successfully, if you have invested the time to get to know your professor, you will be more comfortable requesting a letter of recommendation from them at any time. If they know you well, they will be able to write a strong, lengthy, and detailed letter on your behalf. The more in-depth their testament to the type of student you are is, the stronger their letter of recommendation will be. Some advisors and counselors may be less inclined to write letters for students in a timely manner if they are unfamiliar with them. So you definitely want to reach out to the people in these positions at your school sooner rather than later. Plus, advisors can be extremely useful in providing knowledge about navigating your general or premedical pathway at any stage of the way.

If you never saw the need of having a working relationship with any of these key players at your institution, then perhaps some of these points may have changed your mind. But how do you successfully secure a letter of recommendation you might ask? Below is a list of things to keep in mind before you approach your letter writer.

Getting That Letter 101:

- Identify potential letter writer.
- Ask *in person* if possible (gauge their reaction/body language. This is a sign of their level of enthusiasm for advocating on your behalf).
- What should you ask? Try this: I hope to pursue a career in _______ and I plan on applying to _______ in the _____(timeframe). Given ______ (how you and the letter writer know each other), would you be able to write me a ***strong*** letter of recommendation?
- Follow-up in an email w/ resume & personal statement. Also give them a timeframe (aim for 2-3 weeks before deadline for your LORs).

Student Tips, Tricks, and Frequently Asked Questions

Student Tips, Tricks, and FAQs

In today's world, time management has become everyone's biggest problem. There is always so much to do in a day with seemingly little or no time to accomplish it all. As a pre-med student, time is quite important and is your rarest commodity. Between classes, labs, research, and activities, college can seem like a long four years of delayed gratification all gearing up for that moment when you finally get into medical school.

With all that this journey entails, effective time management skill is crucial if you want to excel in every aspect of your pre-med journey. It is a skill that you can never master perfectly, but you can always continue to improve upon. The first essential step to effective time management as a pre-med student is finding the right balance. As much as you may be overwhelmed with academic activities, try and strike a balance between your study time and leisure. Effective time management skills can make studying for multiple classes much easier and can help eliminate the stress and anxiety related to lack of productivity.

Time management is a conscious decision; you don't just dabble into it. It requires purposeful effort, discipline, and commitment for you to maintain it. The more efficient you are in managing your time, the more organized you will become, and having good organizational skills is an attribute every future physician must cultivate. I'm in no way insinuating that time-management is easy, because from my personal experience I'd say it is definitely a constant struggle (as I used to be the Procrastination Princess). Still, along my journey I have learned some organizational tips that help effectively maximize your time as a student. These tips include:

Use a planner

The first tool that transformed my life as a pre-med student was investing in a good planner. As simple as this may sound, it takes effort and time to stay organized and keep a planner. You will always have a long list of responsibilities as you progress in life and the biggest issue is simply trying to remember them all. There is no denying the fact that sometimes keeping up with the responsibilities of college, coupled with a sprinkle of unplanned activities, can be extremely draining. However, working with a planner make things a lot easier.

Events, dates, meetings, deadlines, class times, and test dates can all run together and snowball into one big pile of stress. However, the added stress can be avoided by simply taking the time to jot down reminders about any upcoming responsibilities or commitments you may have. Take the time to record your "TO-DO'S" on a regular basis; this will go a long way in making sure that you don't cluster up activities all in one day or miss out on the important events. It is more beneficial to spend time planning ahead than to lose time jumping from one unplanned activity to another.

Choose a planner that cannot be easily neglected -- for a quick reminder it should be one that catches your attention easily. Depending on your personal preference and tech savviness, you may opt for a printed planner or a virtual one like Google Calendar or the Tiny Calendar App. With whatever style of planner you choose, make a commitment to update your planner daily in the morning and the evenings before you go to bed. You should strive to keep your planner updated since you can only be as organized as your planner is! Try using specific colors for specific activities or specific types of deadlines; visual aids are super useful as quick "at-a-glance" reminders. If you are not sold on having a handwritten planner, search online for apps or keep lists on your computer or phone to try and stay organized.

Set Your Priorities

Constantly re-addressing your priorities is a great way to ensure you are working efficiently. Every day, you are faced with a lot of choices regarding how you spend your time. Your responsibilities will always keep coming, and it can be quite exhausting trying to accomplish everything. This is why it can be so helpful to make a list of your responsibilities and arrange them based on their priority level.

Readdressing your priorities involves categorizing your responsibilities. Take inventory of all the activities that make up your day—where does each activity specifically fit? Make a distinction between those responsibilities that are important and urgent as well as list things that just need to get done. Each task fits into one of these categories and then you must decide on which task you should tend to first. Personally, when I am faced with so many responsibilities, I love starting with simpler tasks so that I am left with more than enough time to tackle the tedious tasks on the list.

Prioritization: Task List Example

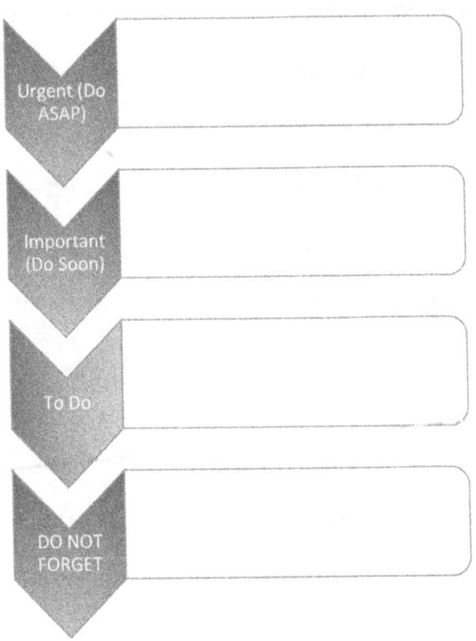

Learning to prioritize your responsibilities is a very important skill. It will be useful not just for now but throughout your whole career. Dealing with patients in the real world requires a constant balance of priorities. You need to develop a good sense of identifying and characterizing problems based on how urgent they are and how much effort you can put into solving them. You must learn to triage your studies and other responsibilities before you can start to triage your future patients.

Avoid Procrastination

Procrastination is the bane of every student's existence, pre-meds included. You know what you should be doing at any given time, but sometimes you just don't want to do it. It is very risky to push off responsibilities and having the "Due later? Do later!" mentality will eventually wear you out. Avoid putting off tasks that you should be focusing and don't let procrastination unknowingly waste your time.

Set your priorities and honor them accordingly. Remind yourself that the best time to carry out any responsibility is usually today! No matter how difficult it might seem, push yourself a little harder to beat procrastination and get what needs to be done, DONE. You will feel less stressed in the long run.

Most pre-meds are perfectionists. So sometimes students procrastinate out of fear of not producing the perfect result. No matter how daunting the task ahead may seem, you can never succeed if you keep pushing it off because eventually you could run out of time and jeopardize the overall quality of your work. Sometimes you need to just start! Procrastination, especially when it comes to essay writing, can be beat by starting with a possible plan and a positive attitude rather than just pushing it off. For example, to fight procrastination with essays I save writing the introduction paragraph for last given the difficulties I had with starting off essays using a perfect opener.

Procrastination is detrimental to your success as a student. Not only can it affect your grades, but it can also convey the message that you are uncommitted and unorganized. The more you procrastinate, the more you are at risk of falling behind on your academic responsibilities. So instead of succumbing to procrastination, work hard and reward yourself with fun and planned breaks.

Rest and Care for Yourself

Amidst school, extracurriculars, and other responsibilities, many pre-med students forget to make time for themselves. Taking care of yourself, or creating time for your personal wellness, is an important aspect of effective time management skills. A major part of learning how to manage one's time revolves around realizing the appropriate times for rest, enjoyment, and socialization. No matter how tight your daily or weekly schedule may seem, find a way to squeeze in wholesome "me time." You can only work at your best when you feel your best, and thus, your personal wellness must be set as a priority as you try to achieve your goals.

"Should I take a break?"

- Have I been studying (really studying) for more than 2 hours straight?
- Am I slowly progressing through or re-reading my work constantly?
- Am I tired? Hungry? Angry? Or have other distracting emotions?
- Break??? No time, too stressed!

How to Take a Break:

- Every 50 to 90 minutes of working take roughly 10-15 minutes to yourself.
- Do something that is not working or studying and that does not require sharp attention/focus.
- Try meditating, coloring, dancing, or exercising. Take a walk, talk with friends, or spend a limited amount of time checking social media.
- Avoid napping for less than 20 minutes as it may make you more tired than you were.

Rest but stick to your study break plan.

As I mentioned countless times, a successful pre-med journey is predicated on finding balance and learning to maximize your time amidst competing priorities. It will be a disaster to embark on your pre-med journey thinking you shouldn't prioritize rest as much as you prioritize meeting your deadlines and assignments. It's okay to take a break so long as you don't quit. Taking a break when necessary does not make you less determined than other people who "grind" all day (and night); you shouldn't feel guilty about it. Being a student is already tough enough; there are times you will feel down, overwhelmed, drained, burnt out and unmotivated. Moments like this are inevitable and they are just another part of your amazing journey to greatness. In such times, remember that self-care is key and it is important to work *smarter* not harder!

The truth is no matter how determined you are, no one can study all the time. There is no use trying because in reality, without your needed breaks, you would lose focus, daydream a bit, and ultimately you wouldn't be effectively studying because of sleep deprivation. The best way to maximize your time as a pre-med student is to practice studying efficiently. The outcome of your study time should be fruitful; set realistic goals for yourself and strive towards achieving them. Re-address your priorities so that you face your studies with 100% focus and determination! Try not to set your rest time or breaks for when you've "learned everything" because you'll never know everything. I am definitely guilty of doing this so believe me when

I tell you it doesn't work. I can tell you from experience that it is important to set SMART goals for studying. Set enough time for breaks and adequate sleep because neglecting this can result in even more stress and anxiety during your studies.

SMART Goals for Studying

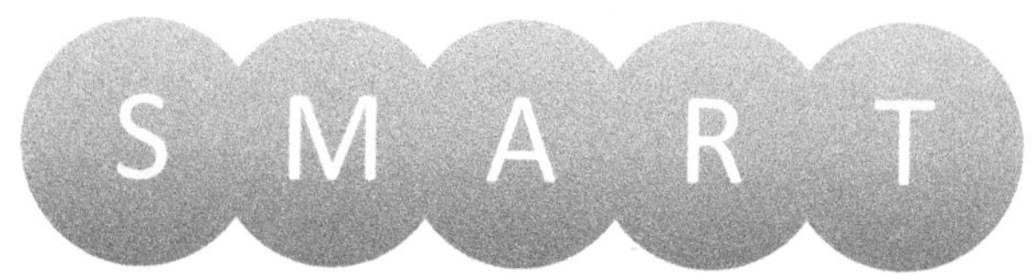

- Specific: *What do you want to achieve?*
- Measurable: *How will you know you finished?*
- Attainable: *Is this something you control?*
- Relevant/Realistic: *Is it worthwhile & realistic?*
- Time-based: *When should you be finished?*

Ex. By 8 p.m., I will have finished 30 practice problems with 75% accuracy rate. (and when I do that, I'll buy myself a coke).

Find time to do the things you love as a way of coping with the inevitable stress. Take a short break, watch your favorite series, hang out with your friends, or go out to that restaurant that you've always longed to visit. Don't forget to check out some cool inspirational medical blogs, or if you are feeling a little bit fancy, treat yourself to a spa date -- you deserve it for all the hard work you've put in so far! Don't allow yourself run empty; you will end up too exhausted to do the things that are actually important.

The tips and FAQs answered over the past few pages will assist you as you navigate your way through your pre-med journey. Always remember, successful time management as a pre-med is not only crucial for getting into medical school, it is incredibly important for the rest of your life. Therefore, make sure you work on your time management skills and maximize your productivity during your designated study hours. Remember, everyone has 24 hours in a day, even Beyoncé. It's only the most successful people that learn to make the most out of them.

Competency Development

Competency Development:

Traits & Characteristics Medical Schools Desire

Competency development is an important part of the pre-medical and medical student journey. The next few pages will outline some of the key competencies, characteristics, and traits that medical schools and residencies seek in future physicians. Use these pages as a time to reflect and highlight your ideals, experiences, and thoughts regarding these competencies. These reflections will be extremely useful for future application writing, committee letters, and interviews, so take these reflective exercises seriously as they can pay off in the future!

Competency Development: Empathy

- What is empathy? And what actions convey it?

Empathy is____

____

____

- How do patients perceive empathetic providers?

____

____

- How does empathy affect the way a physician treats patients?

____

____

- How can you show empathy to others?

____

____

Competency Development: Compassion

- What is compassion? And what actions convey it?

Compassion is ______________________________

____

____

- How do patients perceive compassionate providers?

____

____

- How does compassion affect the way a physician treats patients?

____

____

- How can you show compassion to others?

____

____

Competency Development: Resilience

- What is resilience? And what actions convey it?

Resilience is____

____

____

- How do patients perceive resilient providers?

____

____

- How does resilience affect the way a physician practices?

____

____

- How can you cultivate a sense of resilience?

____

____

Competency Development: Dedication

- What is dedication? And what actions convey it?

Dedication is____

____

____

- How do patients perceive dedicated providers?

____

____

- How does dedication affect the way a physician treats patients?

____

____

- How can you show dedication to others?

____

____

Competency Development: Teamwork

- What comes to mind when thinking of "effective teamwork"? How does it relate to the practice of medicine?

___

___

___

- Reflect on a time you were a part of an effective team.

___

___

- What qualities are needed for effective teamwork?

___

___

- Reflect on a time when a team did not work effectively.

___

___

Competency Development:

Cultural Competency

- Definition:

____

- Why is this important to embody as a future physician?

____

____

Humanism

- Definition:

____

- What does humanism in medicine mean to you?

____

____

- What place does humanism have in the practice of medicine today?

____

____

Rest If You Must, But Don't Quit

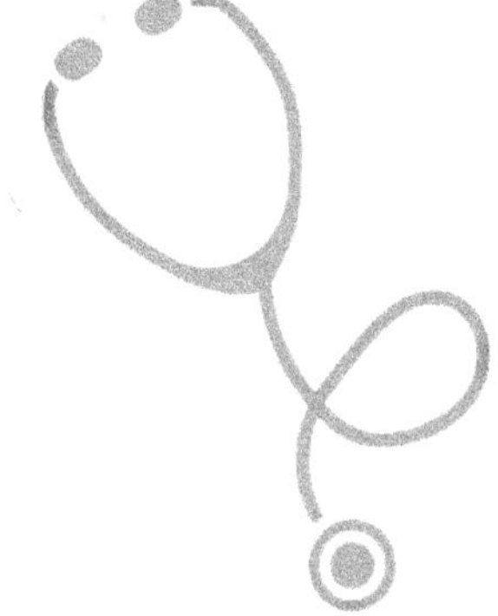

Rest if you must, but don't quit

The pre-med life comes with its unique challenges. These challenges may be mostly academic but there will be many emotional trials along the way. As a medical student hopeful, you might be so driven at times that you forget that there is a life outside of studying. Sometimes we have a tendency to get ahead of ourselves when it comes to pursuing our goals. While this is somewhat commendable, it is equally important to remember that there is only so much we can achieve as a human being in one day.

Successfully going through the pre-medical journey is all about finding the right balance but sometimes the best solution to succeed is to take a break. Many pre-med students are not sold on the idea of self-care. The sad reality is that many people neglect their wellness for the sake of achieving their goals. In our bid to reach milestones, what we fail to acknowledge is that we cannot pour from an empty cup. You must prioritize self-care and treat it is as a necessity rather than as an indulgence.

It is far more beneficial to take breaks when you can than to wait to re-center yourself after you have burned out. The benefits far outweigh the consideration of time wasting that deters you from it. When you prioritize your physical and mental stability above all things, you will have more energy to give your academic work your focus. You will have more energy, you will look forward to every new day of opportunity, and both you and your immune system will be on point! Thus, we must plan for wellness just like we plan out the rest of our life. So I now ask, what does self-care look like for you?

Self-Care _______ (day of the week)

On _______s, I will allow myself to enjoy:

____

____

____

____

Self-Care Contract

I promise to keep my personal wellness and self-care as a priority as I strive to reach my goals each day.

Signed, ________________________________

Self-care is an important part of having a successful career in medicine. As delightful as this sounds, it is not always as easy as it seems to prioritize. From my own experience, I can tell you that pressure can come from every corner as you pursue a career in medicine, and life can sometimes get in the way of your goals, but it should never deter you. Self-care is your own conscious decision, and it is one choice you should always make. Strive toward living a balanced life as a pre-med student, embrace the options and opportunities as they come and don't let yourself get overwhelmed with the pre-med struggle.

Always Remember:

You can't pour from an empty cup; you need to take care of yourself before you can pour into others!

Anti-Wellness Myths

"The Three S's ... you can only have two"

The age old saying goes that successful students are always busy. In #ThePreMedLifestyle, there is not always time to sleep, study, AND have a social life. It is said that a good student can only balance two of these S's. So, with the option of three S's, it's our choice of which two we decide to master.

... which two do you choose?

Circle Two:

Social life   Sleep   Study

Which two do you *actually* master or balance easily?

______________________________ ______________________________

Why is it hard for you to make time for the third S?

____

____

What can you do to make time for all three S's?

____

____

____

____

Stress and Struggles

Stress and Struggles:

Support systems and surrounding yourself with positivity are very important parts of your future success.

Who are the people you can reach out to in your times of need?

Name:____________________ Number: _______________

I can depend on them for: ____________________________

Name:____________________ Number: _______________

I can depend on them for:____________________________

Name:____________________ Number: _______________

I can depend on them for: ____________________________

Stress and Struggles:

Mindfulness

What are some sources of stress and what does stress look like for you?

____

____

____

____

____

____

<u>Mini-Mindfulness Exercise:</u>

- Pause, relax, get into a comfortable position, and close your eyes. STOP THINKING!
- Breathe deeply and become aware of your breath- How long, your chest rise and fall, etc.
- Become aware of your body. Acknowledge each body part and where you are in the room. Open your eyes ☺

Stress and Struggles:

Mindfulness through Mandala drawings

Medically themed mandalas for the perfect pre-med stress relieving color session!

"Wherever the art of medicine is loved, there is also the love of humanity."
-Hippocrates

"Continue Learning.
Never Stop Striving.
And Keep Your
Curiosity SHARP!"

"It's a beautiful thing when a career and passion come together."

"A healthy attitude is contagious, but don't wait to catch it from others. Be a carrier"

-Tom Sheppard

Regardless of what your path to medicine might look like, it is important to remember that everyone's story of success is their own. You may have embarked on this pre-med journey and faced different trials, but that doesn't mean you won't make it through to the end. *Being a pre-med student is hard*, and it is even harder when you don't learn to accept that your path is unique and recognize your strengths and weaknesses from the start. Becoming a successful pre-med student is not 100% based on how well you perform academically; it has a whole lot to do with how well you are prepared mentally and emotionally for any difficulties that might come your way. Stay motivated, always #TreatYourself, and definitely reach out for help and support whenever you may need it.

Remember:

One of the biggest mistakes we can make is undervaluing what we *already* have.

You are capable of attaining anything you put your mind to. Look back at all that you have accomplished over the years and let that be a testament to your greatness and a sign of successes to come. Continue to strive for greatness and *bloom where you are planted.* Everything will work out exactly the way it is supposed to.

- Osaro Obanor

-

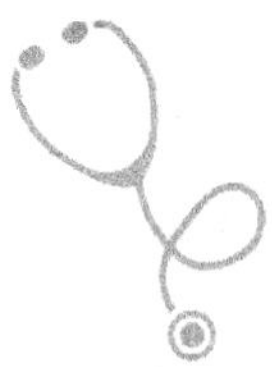

Reflection journal? Planner? On-going to-do list? Notes from a pre-med meeting? Or just doodling to stay awake in Organic Chem? We have you covered! Use this Bullet Journal Section as a space to creatively organize your plans, to-do's, and thoughts along the pre-med journey.

Happy Journaling!

CPSIA information can be obtained
at www.ICGtesting.com
Printed in the USA
FSHW011350281219
65546FS

9 781093 13892